T0413958

Searchlight
BOOKS™

Saving Animals with Science

Protecting Ocean Animals

Lisa Idzikowski

Lerner Publications ◆ Minneapolis

For my family

Lerner Publications Company
An imprint of Lerner Publishing Group, Inc.
241 First Avenue North
Minneapolis, MN 55401 USA

For reading levels and more information, look up this title at www.lernerbooks.com.

Main body text set in Adrianna Regular.
Typeface provided by Chank.

Library of Congress Cataloging-in-Publication Data

Names: Idzikowski, Lisa, author.
Title: Protecting ocean animals / Lisa Idzikowski.
Description: Minneapolis, MN : Lerner Publications, [2024] | Series: Searchlight Books. Saving animals with science ; 01 | Includes bibliographical references and index. | Audience: Ages 8–11 years | Audience: Grades 4–6 | Summary: "Ocean pollution is just one of many problems that afflict ocean animals. Readers learn how science is working to help cut down on ocean pollution and overfishing and to increase conservation efforts"— Provided by publisher.
Identifiers: LCCN 2023010617 (print) | LCCN 2023010618 (ebook) | ISBN 9798765609156 (lib. bdg.) | ISBN 9798765624807 (pbk.) | ISBN 9798765617267 (epub)
Subjects: LCSH: Marine sciences—Juvenile literature. | Marine animals—Conservation—Juvenile literature. | Marine habitat conservation—Juvenile literature. | Marine resources conservation—Juvenile literature. | BISAC: JUVENILE NONFICTION / Animals / Animal Welfare
Classification: LCC GC21.5 .I3 2024 (print) | LCC GC21.5 (ebook) | DDC 333.91/6416—dc23/eng20230715

LC record available at https://lccn.loc.gov/2023010617
LC ebook record available at https://lccn.loc.gov/2023010618

Manufactured in the United States of America
1-1009624-51593-5/18/2023

Table of Contents

Chapter 1

GREAT BIG OCEAN

In 2022, scientists sent a drone to follow a sei whale and her calf. When the drone got close, it dropped a biologging tag onto the mother to track her movements.

Sei whales are on the endangered species list. Not much is known about them. The tag will help scientists learn more about these whales. This includes their

A drone flying
over the ocean

behavior, migration patterns, and how they interact
with their habitat. Scientists hope that by knowing more
about these animals, they can better protect them.

Fish swimming in a coral reef

Giant Watery World

Oceans cover almost three-quarters of the planet. They provide food, make half of Earth's oxygen, and help control our planet's climate. A healthy ocean is important for life on Earth.

But pollution, overfishing, and damage to marine habitats hurt Earth's oceans. This puts sea life populations in danger. Tagging ocean animals is just one way that scientists are trying to help. Every day, people are finding new ways to use science to keep our oceans and its animals healthy.

Spotlight On
Geoff Shester

Geoff Shester is the California campaign director at Oceana, a conservation organization. Every year, climate change is putting Earth's oceans at risk. That's why marine researchers such as Shester study ocean life in hopes of keeping oceans healthy. Using his robot Gino, special cameras, and other technology, Shester works to help save the ocean.

Gino is an underwater drone like this one.

Chapter 2

OCEAN POLLUTION

Pollution is a big problem in our oceans. But what is it? Discover ocean pollution, its effects on ocean animals, and how science is trying to prevent it.

Plastic Pollution

Ocean pollution happens when humans release harmful things, such as oil, plastic, and other waste, into the ocean. But plastic is one of the biggest problems.

Over 8.8 million tons (8.0 million t) of plastic enters the ocean each year. Sea animals are at great risk due to plastic pollution.

A Stellar Study

In July 2022, a Steller's sea lion got its neck trapped inside a plastic packing strap. Three boats raced to the scene off the coast of Washington State. Veterinarians gave

FLOATING GARBAGE ON THE SEA
▼

A sea lion tangled up in plastic packaging material

the 500-pound (227-kg) mammal medicine to slow its movements so the animal wouldn't hurt itself when they crept close to help. The crew cut the plastic packing strap to free the sea lion.

Plastic pollution can be deadly for ocean critters. Every year, over one hundred thousand ocean animals die from eating or getting tangled in plastic. That's why science is finding new ways to tackle this issue.

Recycling

Recycling helps keep plastic out of the ocean. Instead of being dumped in landfills or ocean waters, plastic gets shuffled into processing facilities. Then it is sorted and made into new products at other facilities.

Scientists are looking at ways to improve recycling. One way is called enzymatic recycling. Enzymes are a type of protein and are present in all living organisms. In 2020, scientists created a super enzyme that can "eat" certain types of plastic. These super enzymes break down plastic faster and more efficiently than regular recycling. Scientists hope that one day, super enzymes might be used to "eat" plastic already in the ocean.

Recycling facilities crush plastic into large cubes.

The H2OPE River Whale is a cleanup machine that picks up trash in rivers before it reaches oceans.

Ocean Cleanup

But the ocean doesn't have to wait for super enzymes to catch up. The Floating Robot for Eliminating Debris is a slow-moving, solar-powered robot that floats in the ocean. It collects garbage in the water, including floating plastic. To make sure the robot doesn't harm ocean life, it uses sound to alert animals that it's coming.

Seabin also cleans up the ocean. This floating trash bin collects plastic and other garbage from the water using a filter. It sucks in water like a sinkhole. Any water sucked in is cleaned and flows back out, leaving trash inside the bin.

PEOPLE CAN DO THEIR PART
BY CLEANING UP BEACHES
AND RECYCLING.

Chapter 3

CONSERVATION OF OCEANS

One way to protect ocean animals is by protecting the home they live in. Discover how scientists are taking care of ocean habitats, rebuilding coral reefs, and more!

Marine Protected Areas

Many living creatures make their home in the ocean. But what protections do they have?

In 2022, leaders from around the world met at a climate conference. Many countries in attendance, including the US, voiced their support for the 30x30 project. This project aims to conserve at least 30 percent of the world's land and ocean by 2030. It will create marine protected areas (MPAs), which will be like national parks. People won't be allowed to drill for oil there. Some MPAs also do not allow fishing. This gives ocean life a safe place to live or recover their populations. Many MPAs are already in place around the world. But the 30x30 project means there will be more.

Ang Thong National Marine Park in Thailand is an MPA.

When coral is stressed, it turns white and is at risk of dying.

Coral Reefs

Coral reefs are home to around four thousand species of fish. But climate change, pollution, and overfishing are causing coral reefs to die. About 50 percent of the world's coral reefs have been lost, and more could die out.

But science is helping reefs bounce back. Researchers studying the ocean know that coral reefs in MPAs can recover from human-made problems. Other scientists are bringing reefs back to life by regrowing coral and reintroducing it to the ocean.

Spotlight On
Mote Marine Laboratory and Aquarium

In Florida, researchers at the Mote Marine Laboratory and Aquarium keep busy. Florida's Coral Reef has lost over 90 percent of its living coral. To help, scientists breed coral that are resistant to, or not affected by, disease. Then they plant the healthy coral back into the damaged reefs. Every year, Mote scientists successfully plant thousands of these farmed corals.

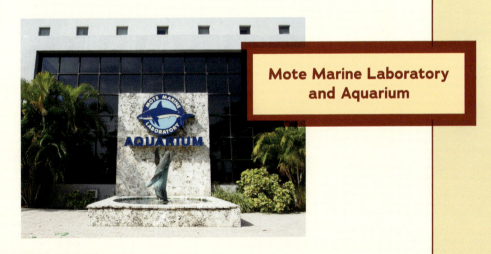

Mote Marine Laboratory and Aquarium

A tag on a whale shark swimming off the coast of Africa

Tagging Marine Animals

Biologging tags are used to study an animal's movements and behaviors. They are especially helpful for scientists to learn more about endangered animals.

The Galapagos Whale Shark Project is one example of scientists using biologging tags to help protect sea life. This project aims to learn more about the habits and movements of whale sharks, which are an endangered species. In 2022, the group tagged their first whale shark south of the Galápagos Islands. Scientists hope that by studying whale sharks and conserving the area they live in, there will be more whale sharks.

The Galápagos Islands is home to one of the largest MPAs in the world.

Chapter 4

OCEAN FISHING

Fishing is a big industry. But is it harmful? Discover how ships, fishing tools, and overfishing affect ocean populations, and what technology is doing to save it.

What's Wrong with Fishing?

Over three billion people around the world eat fish as a source of protein. People can make a lot of money fishing. But sometimes, fishers catch too many fish. Ocean life, such as turtles or whales, can also get caught or tangled in fishing gear meant for other creatures. This is called bycatch.

Turtle Filter

Technology is trying to lessen bycatch. For example, fishers often use large nets to catch shrimp. Sometimes they accidentally scoop up turtles. A turtle excluder device helps sea turtles escape these nets. It is a metal grid placed inside the net, and it acts like a filter. Small shrimp pass through, but sea turtles use the metal grid to escape.

Turtle filters mean fewer turtles will be accidentally caught.

Sharks can avoid becoming bycatch when fishers use SharkGuard.

Keeping Sharks Away

SharkGuard is a small tool that can be attached to long lines. It sends out electrical signals that sharks can sense. These electrical signals do not hurt the sharks, but they do not like them. Sharks that feel these electrical signals will avoid the fishing lines.

Ghost Gear

Ghost gear, or fishing gear that gets lost or left in the ocean, is also a problem for fish. Fish can get caught or trapped in ghost gear. Biodegradable nets, or nets that break down naturally over time, help keep fish safe. So does adding tracking devices onto gear.

LOST FISHING NET ON A CORAL REEF

Deep Dive
ReShark

Almost 40 percent of shark and ray species are at risk of dying out. ReShark is a global group trying to restore sharks in Earth's oceans. They take eggs of endangered shark species and hatch them in a research and conservation center. Then the sharks are looked after by human "shark nannies" and later released into the wild. In early 2023, ReShark released two zebra sharks into the waters around Indonesia.

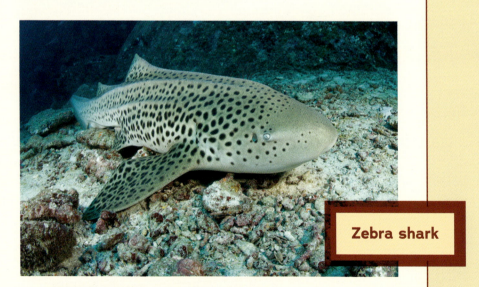

Zebra shark

Overfishing

Overfishing has been a problem since the 1800s. Overfishing is when fishers take fish out of the ocean faster than new fish are born. Bluefin tuna have been greatly overfished, as have whales, the Atlantic cod, and even sharks.

To prevent overfishing, fishing rules limit fishers to catch only certain types and sizes of fish. That way, fishing doesn't affect just one type of fish, and fish will not be caught until they're full-grown adults. Following these rules gives fish a chance to have babies and grow.

A commercial fishing boat hauling in its net

Deep Dive
Whale Safe

Ship strikes are when ships hit whales. Whale Safe is a near real-time map that shows where whales are swimming so people can avoid them. It combines several technologies. It uses an underwater microphone that picks up whale calls in the ocean. It also uses whale sightings people have reported through an app. Scientists combine this information with data gathered through biologging tags to predict where whales will likely be. This creates a map that ships can use to avoid whales.

Whales swimming next to a boat

Boats also use LED lights.

Flashing Lights

A system called Pisces is helping fish too. This LED light system can be clipped onto fishing nets. It sets off different colored lights underwater. Different lights, colors, and patterns attract different types of fish. By mixing the settings, fishers can attract certain fish while avoiding others.

Protecting Marine Life

Protecting the ocean and all its living creatures is a big job. But scientists are always coming up with new ideas, technology, and ways to make it possible!

Save the Day

Over 80 percent of the world's oceans remain unexplored and unknown. By exploring the ocean, scientists learn about its fish, plants, and more. Studying these things helps scientists find more ways to save the ocean. Robotics and artificial intelligence are already helping scientists by exploring the ocean's depths. What other ways might science and technology help scientists save the ocean?

Glossary

bycatch: marine life caught when fishing for a different species

climate change: significant, long-lasting change in Earth's climate and weather due to global warming

conservation: protection of something

drone: an aircraft that is piloted remotely or automatically by computers

endangered: an animal or plant at risk of dying out

habitat: the place or environment where a plant or animal lives and grows

LED: short for a light-emitting diode, or a device that lets off light when electricity flows through it

marine: having to do with the ocean

overfishing: catching fish faster than they can reproduce, putting their future population at risk

species: a group of organisms with similar attributes

Learn More

Hamby, Rachel. *Restoring the Great Barrier Reef.* Lake Elmo, MN: Focus Readers, 2020.

Hyde, Natalie. *Preventing Ocean Pollution.* New York: Crabtree, 2021.

National Geographic Kids: Ocean Habitat
https://kids.nationalgeographic.com/nature/habitats/article/ocean

National Geographic Kids: Plastic Pollution
https://kids.nationalgeographic.com/nature/kids-vs-plastic/article/pollution-1

National Ocean Service: How Can You Help Our Ocean?
https://oceanservice.noaa.gov/ocean/help-our-ocean.html

Walker, Tracy Sue. *Saving Endangered Species.* Minneapolis: Lerner Publications, 2024.

Index

Photo Acknowledgments

Image Credits: Phuwadach Pattanatmon/Shutterstock, p. 5; Georgette Douwma/Getty Images, p. 6; Massimo Parisi/Alamy, p. 7; mbala mbala merlin/iStockphoto/Getty Images, p. 9; Mauro Toccaceli/Alamy, p. 10; Erik Isakson/Getty Images, p. 11; Andia/Universal Images Group/Getty Images, p. 12; Alistair Berg/Getty Images, p. 13; banjongseal324/Getty Images, p. 15; Richard Whitcombe/Shutterstock, p. 16; Katharine Andriotis/Alamy, p. 17; ullstein bild/Getty Images, p. 18; Rene Holtslag/Shutterstock, p. 19; Jeff Rotman/Alamy Stock Photo, p. 21; Andrew Thirlwell/Getty Images, p. 22; Reinhard Dirscherl/Corbis/Getty Images, p. 23; Stuart Westmorland/Getty Images, p. 24; taylanibrahim/Getty Images, p. 25; bernard radvaner/Getty Images, p. 26; Aleksandra Koska/Alamy, p. 27; Patrick J. Endres/Getty Images, p. 28.

Cover: Giordano Cipriani/The Image Bank/Getty Images.